What was Jesus' Message?

STUDIES IN CREATIVE CRITICISM

What was Jesus' Message?

J. C. FENTON

LONDON   SPCK   1971

*First published in 1971
by S.P.C.K.
Holy Trinity Church
Marylebone Road
London NW1 4DU*

*Made and printed in Great Britain by
The Talbot Press (S.P.C.K.), Saffron Walden Essex*
12858

SBN 281 02621 **1**

CONTENTS

ACKNOWLEDGEMENTS

Quotations from the *Revised Standard Version* of the Bible, copyrighted 1946 and 1952 by the Division of Christian Education of the National Council of Churches of Christ in the United States of America, are used by permission.

The extract on page 11 from *Jesus Rediscovered* by Malcolm Muggeridge (Collins 1969) is reproduced by permission.

PREFACE

The main part of this book (chapters 1–5) consists of lectures delivered at the Vacation Term for Biblical Study at Oxford, 12–15 August 1969; chapter 6 is a revised and abbreviated version of an address given in the chapel of Cuddesdon Theological College on the evening of 15 August 1969. I would like to take this opportunity of thanking the executive committee of the Vacation Term for their kind invitation to deliver the lectures, and the then Principal of Cuddesdon, now Bishop of St Albans, for asking me to preach to the college.

In preparing the manuscript for publication I have left it very much in the style in which it was originally composed for oral delivery, in the hope that though this has obvious disadvantages it may also have some compensating advantages. It would, in theory at least, have been possible, for example, to add footnotes to almost every sentence in the lectures, thus providing sources and authorities for nearly every statement that is made: there is nothing original here. Similarly, and perhaps this is more important, it would have been possible to quote views which are totally opposed to those which are here expressed. But it seemed to me that, if the lectures had any value, it lay in putting forward one point of view on a complicated and much discussed subject in a way that would not over-burden the reader. I am not so naive as to think either that this is the only point of view on this subject, or that it will not cause offence.

We live in an age of rapid change, as we are often told, and this is true of New Testament study no less than of other areas of life. On some points I might express myself now in a slightly different manner; but on the whole I think that I would still maintain the basic positions for which I attempted to argue then.

I should perhaps add one further reflection: Most of what I tried to say in the summer of 1969 is said with far greater learning and much more grace by John Austin Baker in *The Foolishness of God* (Darton, Longman and Todd 1970), particularly in Part Two, Jesus of Nazareth.

St Chad's College, Durham   JOHN FENTON

1 INTRODUCTION

Three reasons have led to the writing of this book:

1. First, it had often seemed to me that the students with whom I was working had no clear idea what Jesus said. These students were ordination candidates of the Church of England, and so not completely unacquainted with the New Testament. If they could not say, in their own words, what Jesus' message was, then it might be that there were others, too, who were unclear about it; for example, their parish clergy, their schoolmasters, their Sunday School teachers.

One of the ways in which I had discovered this uncertainty was like this: I would say to a student during a tutorial: "If I were to say to you, Darwin, you might reply, Evolution. And if I were to say, Marx, you might reply, Communism. And if I were to say, Freud, you might say, Psychoanalysis. Then if I said, Jesus, what would you say?"

In the majority of cases this produced no answer at all. But sometimes a man suggested Christianity, which deserves a gamma plus: it is certainly not completely wrong, but it is not very good. You can scarcely say that Jesus taught Christianity; if Christianity is faith in one who died and rose again, this is not what Jesus taught. And there is another sense in which it is wrong: Darwin, I imagine, used the word Evolution, and Marx Communism, and Freud Psychoanalysis; but Jesus, so far as we know, never used a word which could be translated Christianity. Christianity was not the key term in the teaching of Jesus, as those others were in the teaching of Darwin, Marx, and Freud.

2. Secondly, when I was an undergraduate at Oxford in the early 1940s I neither had any clear ideas about the message of Jesus nor did I think it right, or possible, or desirable, to have them. My teacher, the late R. H. Lightfoot, did not encourage

us to think that we could know much about Jesus. And in this matter I did not need encouraging. I had come up to the university direct (as far as theology was concerned) from Sunday School; we had not studied the subject at my boarding school. And Sunday School had left me with a strong dislike of Jesus. Therefore I rejoiced at being told that the Gospels contained little more than a whisper of his voice, and I contrived to pass the honour school without touching questions on the historical Jesus, if there were any.

Things have changed since then, and now we are told by some scholars that we can know about Jesus, and that it is possible to form some ideas as to what he said. Moreover, what they are saying on this subject now is very different from what I was told in Sunday School. Writing this book has been an attempt to clarify my own mind.

3. The third reason will seem old-fashioned to many people. One of the reasons whoy nineteenth-century writers were interested in the historical Jesus was because they suspected that the movement which he started had gone wrong at some point—some said as early as Paul. They were hoping to get back to a more pure and simple Christianity, by getting behind the Church, to Jesus as he was.

I thought there might still be something in this. Could it be the case, I wondered, that the ways of thinking and talking about Jesus which started with Paul (or earlier, with the pre-Pauline Hellenistic Church) and continued with John and the author of Hebrews, had now run out of energy? Certainly something seemed to have run out of energy: biblical ways of talking about Jesus did not seem to appeal and convert, as they had done until only a decade or two before. Might it be that we had come to the end of an era which began with the apostles and that, to make Jesus mean anything now, we had to approach him, not through the traditional doctrines of the Church, but through the ways provided for us by historical criticism of the Gospels?

And there was one argument that fitted in here and made me think that this must be so. I had always believed in providence.

If there were a God worth believing, he ought to be doing things; and if he were doing anything, he ought to be doing everything; so it should be possible to see everything as providential. If this was so, what was providential about the emergence of historical criticism of the Gospels—if it was not in order that we might have a new understanding of Jesus, and so a renewed Christianity?

This seemed to be Mr Muggeridge's position also:

I believe, as it is written in the New Testament, that if we would save our lives we must lose them; that we cannot live by bread alone; that we must die in the flesh to be reborn in the spirit, and that the flesh lusts contrary to the spirit and the spirit contrary to the flesh; that God cannot see a sparrow fall to the ground without concern, and has counted the hairs of each head, so that all that lives deserves our respect and reverence, and no one man can conceivably be more important, of greater significance, or in any way more deserving of consideration than any other. God is our father, we are his children, and so one family, brothers and sisters together.

It is true that these basic propositions of Christianity have got cluttered up with dogma of various kinds which I find often incomprehensible, irrelevant, and even repugnant. All the same, I should be proud and happy to be able to call myself a Christian; to dare to measure myself against that sublimely high standard of human values and human behaviour.[1]

In the former paragraph of this quotation, there are possible allusions to seven passages in the New Testament (Mark 8. 35; Matt. 4. 4=Luke 4. 4 (quoting Deut. 8. 3);? John 3. 3f; Gal. 5. 17; Matt. 10. 29; Matt. 10. 30; Mark 3. 35), of which six are in the four Gospels. Was it not the case that the Christianity which meant something to Mr Muggeridge was the message of Jesus, and not the dogma of various kinds that came in with Paul and the others? Was not this why he gave his book the title *Jesus Rediscovered*?

These, then, were the reasons which led to my writing: it seemed to be a subject about which there was some ignorance in quarters where you might not have expected ignorance; my desire to clarify my own mind; and the possibility that in this

[1] Malcolm Muggeridge, *Jesus Rediscovered* (Collins, 1969), p. 56.

area above all we might find ideas which would help us to make
sense of Jesus to ourselves and our contemporaries.

It may help the reader if at this point there is a statement of
certain critical positions which have been adopted and for which
no arguments will be given here; if the reader is puzzled by
them, he will have to consult the standard works on the subject (e.g. W. G. Kümmel, *Introduction to the New Testament*.
S.C.M. 1966). There are four such assumptions:

1. In reconstructing the message of Jesus, we should ignore
the Gospel according to John. It may be that the author of
this Gospel knew and made use of genuine sayings of Jesus
which had been passed on to him from the earliest times but
had not been recorded by the other three evangelists. However,
it is extremely difficult to identify such sayings now, and in my
view there are not many of them.

2. Mark is earlier than Matthew or Luke, and was used by
them. Therefore in those passages which appear in both Mark
and Matthew, or in both Mark and Luke, we shall follow the
Marcan form as the one which is more likely to be original.

3. The stories about Jesus, and his sayings, were preserved
and handed on in the oral period, before the Gospels were
written, in small units; and these units were assembled by the
evangelists, who had no information as to their relative dates,
i.e. whether they belonged to the early, middle, or later part of
the ministry of Jesus.

4. Finally, these units of tradition were used by Christians in
the oral period, and by the evangelists when they put them together to form their Gospels, to express their post-Easter faith
in Jesus as the Lord and Messiah; and this use of the material
has left a deposit on it which must be removed if we want to see
the tradition in its original form.[1]

[1] A good example of this process of removing the over-painting which
was done by the early Church can be found in J. Jeremias, *The Parables of
Jesus* (S.C.M., 1963), part II, The Return to Jesus from the Primitive
Church; for a simplified version of this, see J. Jeremias, *Rediscovering
the Parables* (S.C.M., 1966), pp. 16-88.

2 "THE KINGDOM OF GOD IS AT HAND"

If we are right in thinking that the evangelists used material which came to them in separate units, and that this material had already been coated with the faith of the communities (see (3) and (4) above p. 12), then our problem is to find a thread or pattern in the tradition which will help us to make sense of it.

Our way of doing this—and it is the way we shall follow now—is to take a summary of the message of Jesus which one of the evangelists provides. It is the earliest of the evangelists who gives it, and it is as follows:

Now after John was arrested, Jesus came into Galilee, preaching the gospel of God, and saying, "The time is fulfilled, and the kingdom of God is at hand; repent, and believe in the gospel."
(Mark 1. 14f)

We are starting with this passage, not because it is thought that it contains an original saying of Jesus (it is probably Mark's own wording), but for lack of any better starting-point. And we shall take it provisionally, as an hypothesis; asking, Does this summary act as the thread we need in order to make sense of the tradition? Does the material begin to fall into a shape, around this theme?

But immediately we run into two difficulties: 1. What is meant by the expression, The kingdom of God? 2. What is the meaning of the verb (ἤγγικεν) which is translated "is at hand" in the RSV, but which some scholars have said should be rendered "has arrived"? That is to say, does it mean, "is nearly here"?— or does it mean, "has come and now is"?

Both these difficulties have been discussed at great length and in great detail, and we shall not go into that now. We shall, however, notice two points both of which seem to be clear, and both of which seem to be important.

13

1. First, Jesus is here made to say something like this: "You are in a particular situation; and in this situation, the approprate action to take is this". That is the kind of saying Mark is putting into the mouth of Jesus at this point; and one can think of many other examples of sayings of this kind; e.g.

> The ship is sinking: man the life-boats!
> The staircase is on fire: jump out of the window!
> Tea is ready: come and get it!

In each of these examples the saying is made up of two sentences; this is what they have in common. The first sentence contains a verb in the indicative (is) which describes the situation; the second sentence contains a verb in the imperative (man, jump, come, get) which describes what is appropriate in the situation.

Similarly, in Mark 1. 15 there are two verbs in the indicative (is fulfilled, is at hand), and two in the imperative (repent, believe). It may be that in each case the second verb describes more fully or defines more closely the meaning of the first; thus "the kingdom of God is at hand" defines and explains what is meant by "the time is fulfilled"; and "believe in the gospel" defines and explains what is meant by the somewhat vague word "repent" (see below, p. 22).

We shall return to this basic structure of indicative and imperative, situation and command, later on; meanwhile there is a second point which emerges from Mark's summary of the message of Jesus.

2. The expression which Mark uses here, in order to describe the situation in which the hearers of Jesus found themselves, is "the kingdom of God". This expression comes again and again in the tradition of the words of Jesus. In Matthew it usually appears in the form "the kingdom of heaven", but that means precisely the same as "the kingdom of God", because heaven is a devout periphrasis for God. There are about a hundred instances of these expressions in the synoptic Gospels; and the way in which they are used shows that this is the dominant or key idea in the message of Jesus. Therefore the answer to the question (see above, p. 9)—Darwin, Evolution; Marx, Com-

munism; Freud, Psychoanalysis; Jesus, what?—should be, The kingdom of God.

The question we must now ask is, Does the pattern of Mark 1. 15 (i.e. indicative and imperative; situation and command) provide us with a clue to what was the main theme in the message of Jesus? Does much of the material fall into this pattern? We started with Mark 1. 15 only in a provisional way, using it as an hypothesis; we must now test it on the material.

THE PARABLES

The part of the material to take first is the parables, because they are stories, and stories of this kind are less easily changed than isolated sayings; and because, when they have been changed by the Church in the oral period, the changes are fairly easy to detect and to undo; the parables give us the best and most reliable information concerning the message of Jesus.

Here are ten parables; and in each of them a picture is presented of a person in a situation in which, if he is wise, he will act in an appropriate manner; but if he is not wise, he will not.

1. As you go with your accuser before the magistrate, make an effort to settle with him on the way, lest he drag you to the judge, and the judge hand you over to the officer, and the officer put you in prison.   *(Luke 12. 58)*

2. The kingdom of heaven is like treasure hidden in a field, which a man found and covered up; then in his joy he goes and sells all that he has and buys that field.   *(Matt. 13. 44)*

3. The kingdom of heaven is like a merchant in search of fine pearls, who, on finding one pearl of great value, went and sold all that he had and bought it.   *(Matt. 13. 45f)*

4. The kingdom of heaven may be compared to a king who wished to settle accounts with his servants. When he began the reckoning, one was brought to him who owed him ten thousand talents; and as he could not pay, his lord ordered him to be sold, with his wife and children and all that he had, and payment to be made. So the servant fell on his knees, imploring him, 'Lord, have patience with me, and I will pay you everything'. And out of pity for him the Lord of that servant released him and forgave him the debt. . .   *(Matt. 18. 23f)*

5. There was a rich man who had a steward, and charges were brought to him that this man was wasting his goods. And he

2

called him and said to him, 'What is this that I hear about you? Turn in the account of your stewardship, for you can no longer be steward'. And the steward said to himself, 'What shall I do, since my master is taking the stewardship away from me? I am not strong enough to dig, and I am ashamed to beg. I have decided what to do, so that people may receive me into their houses when I am put out of the stewardship.' . . *(Luke 16. 1f)*

6. The kingdom of heaven may be compared to a king who gave a marriage feast for his son, and sent his servants to call those who were invited to the marriage feast; but they would not come. Again he sent other servants, saying, 'Tell those who were invited, Behold, I have made ready my dinner, my oxen and my fat calves are killed, and everything is ready; come to the marriage feast.' . .   *(Matt. 22. 1f)*

7. Know this, that if the householder had known in what part of the night the thief was coming, he would have watched and would not have let his house be broken into.   *(Matt. 23. 43)*

8. The kingdom of heaven shall be compared to ten maidens who took their lamps and went to meet the bridegroom. Five of them were foolish, and five were wise. For when the foolish took their lamps, they took no oil with them; but the wise took flasks of oil with their lamps. As the bridegroom was delayed, they all slumbered and slept. But at midnight there was a cry, 'Behold, the bridegroom! Come out to meet him.' . .   *(Matt. 25. 1f)*

9. It will be as when a man going on a journey called his servants and entrusted to them his property; to one he gave five talents, to another two, to another one, to each according to his ability. Then he went away. . . . Now after a long time the master of those servants came and settled accounts with them. . .
                                                (Matt. 25. 14f)

10. There was a rich man, who was clothed in purple and fine linen and who feasted sumptuously every day. And at his gate lay a poor man named Lazarus, full of sores, who desired to be fed with what fell from the rich man's table; moreover the dogs came and licked his sores. . .   *(Luke 16. 19)*

In each of these ten parables, we are presented with a story of people in a situation that calls for action. Sometimes the people in the story take the appropriate action: reconciliation; selling everything; asking for pity; making friends; having a supply of oil; making use of talents. Sometimes they do not act: ignoring the invitation; not watching for the burglar; not having oil with them; feasting every day.

And it would not be difficult to find more parables which have the same basic pattern—e.g. the Rich Fool (Luke 12. 16f), the Doorkeeper (Mark 13. 34f), the Last Judgement (Matt. 25. 31f).

It is therefore beginning to look as though the key which Mark provided in his summary of the message of Jesus (Mark 1. 15) fits the material. The parables—or at least a large proportion of them—contain this pattern of a situation which demands appropriate action.

THE KINGDOM OF GOD IS AT HAND

We can now return to two points we left earlier on. When we first considered Mark 1. 15 (p. 13), we noted that there were two difficulties there: (i) the meaning of The kingdom of God; (ii) the meaning of the verb (ἤγγικεν) which is translated "is at hand" in the RSV. We are now in a position to say something about both of these problems.

If we look at the ten parables on pages 15-16 again, and see how the situations in these stories are described, and the images which are used in order to describe them, we shall understand what is meant by "The time is fulfilled and the kingdom of God is at hand".

The images which point to the situations are as follows:
1. The law court
2. A treasure
3. A pearl
4. A king settling accounts
5. A rich man settling accounts
6. A wedding feast
7. A thief in the night
8. A wedding
9. A rich man settling accounts
10. Death and judgement.

The point is that almost all of these images are used elsewhere to describe the last judgement and the life of the age to come. The law court, the settling of accounts, the king, stand for the last judgement. The thief in the night stands for the coming of the end of the world. The treasure, the pearl of great value, the wedding feast, are all images of the life of the age to come.

Therefore, what Jesus meant when he said (according to Mark) "the kingdom of God is at hand" was "the end of this age is near, and the beginning of the age to come; the last judgement will happen soon".

That this is the right understanding of "the kingdom of God is at hand" is clear from a great deal of evidence elsewhere in the tradition which supports this conclusion.

1. There are *sayings* of Jesus concerning the kingdom of God and entry into it which make it evident beyond question that to enter the kingdom is to enter the life of the age to come; for example,

It is better for you to enter life maimed than with two hands to go to hell, to the unquenchable fire. . . .
It is better for you to enter life lame than with two feet to be thrown into hell. . . .
It is better for you to enter the kingdom of God with one eye than with two eyes to be thrown into hell, where their worm does not die, and the fire is not quenched.   *(Mark 9. 43f)*

Notice here that "life" and "the kingdom of God" are used as parallel synonymous expressions; and that both of them are contrasted with Hell—the fire which is not quenched. There are only two alternatives: either to enter the life of the age to come (that is, the kingdom of God) or to go to hell.

2. It is also clear from the *miracles* of Jesus that the kingdom of God meant for him the life of the age to come. He healed people, as a sign that Satan's time of power was coming to an end, and that God was about to rule. See, for example, the controversy with the scribes in Mark 3. 22f. and parallels, and notice in particular this saying:

But if it is by the finger of God that I cast out demons, then the kingdom of God has come upon you.
                                          (Luke 11. 20, cf. Matt. 12. 28)

The kingdom of God means the time when God will rule. He will rule over the whole of his creation—heaven and earth; man and beast; atmosphere and vegetation. Jesus interpreted his miracles as signs that God's rule was beginning; Satan was bound and his goods (i.e. the sick) were being plundered.

The words of Jesus, and the actions of Jesus, fitted together into a unity; his actions (i.e. the healing miracles) were evidence for the truth of what he said. He said, God is going to rule; and the miracles showed that this was beginning to happen. The miracles were signs of the end of the age.

3. Apparently this is also the conclusion which you would expect from a consideration of the Jewish sources. The kingdom of God is a technical term found in Jewish apocalyptic literature, meaning the time of the age to come. There is no evidence that Jesus discussed the meaning of this expression, either with his followers, or with his opponents. He is never recorded as saying, "When I say The Kingdom of God, I mean something different from what others mean when they use this term". He used it, assuming that he and they meant the same thing when they used it.

CONCLUSION AND FOOTNOTES

The conclusion which we have now reached is very simple and straightforward. It is that the basic theme in the message of Jesus was, The time is fulfilled and the kingdom of God is at hand; and that by this he meant, The end of this age is upon you; the last judgement is coming soon. That was the situation which was depicted in many of the parables; and the parables also contained explanations of the command, which is the other part of Mark's summary, Repent, and believe in the gospel. We shall go on to look at this in the next section.

Meanwhile, three footnotes to this chapter will be appropriate at this point:

1. If the basic theme of Jesus was the imminence of the end, it is unlikely that Jesus said anything about other matters. If you believe that time is running out, and that the last judgement is coming soon, this does not leave you with much else to care about. It is, by its nature, an all-consuming idea. We shall therefore not expect to find in the message of Jesus ideas that are not related to this.

2. People have often resisted the conclusion to which we have come, because, if it were the right conclusion, then it must be said that Jesus was wrong. In fact, the end did not come then, and has still not come. But is it necessary to resist the conclusion that Jesus was wrong? If he was a first century man, should we not expect him to have thought as many first century men also thought? What access had he to ideas, other than through his parents, teachers, contemporaries, the scriptures, and his own conscience? All the evidence is that he shared the raw material of his thinking with his contemporaries. What is significant is what he did with this raw material, as we shall see later.

3. We might, as was suggested above (see pp. 10f), have approached this subject with the hope that the message of Jesus would help us in our present situation more than the ideas of Paul, John, the author of Hebrews, and their followers. If so, the conclusion which we have now reached may seem to be disappointing. Clearly it will not be possible to return to Jesus in a simple and literal sense, if his basic theme was the coming of the end—since the end did not come. If Jesus' message is to be of any help to us today, it will have to be interpreted; a simple reconstruction of it would be useless.

3 "REPENT AND BELIEVE IN THE GOSPEL"

We turn now to the second part of Mark's summary of the message of Jesus, that is to say, to the two imperatives, Repent and Believe. How far does this summary provide a key to the teaching of Jesus?

It will be useful, first, to look again at some of the other examples of the basic Marcan pattern, situation and command; indicative and imperative. For instance, there was the example, The ship is sinking: man the life-boats. The command (Man the life-boats) is implied by the statement of the situation (The ship is sinking); and if the crew and passengers know their drill there will be no need to add the command; the plain statement that the ship is sinking will be adequate. Thus in certain circumstances, a statement by itself has the force of a command; e.g. Tea is ready means Wash your hands and assemble.

It could be therefore that Jesus simply said, The end is near; God is about to rule. He might have been a prophet announcing the imminence of the kingdom. However, when we look at the tradition of his sayings, this does not seem to have been the case. Apparently he did not think that the bare statement of the situation was enough by itself. He did tell people what to do, in view of the approach of the end. And this is probably important: because it may be what he said in his imperatives that created the opposition between the Jewish religious leaders and himself, not what he said in his indicatives. They would not have hated him, or have had him put to death, if he had said no more than, The end is here. Many people at the time believed that the end was near, and they were not hated or executed for saying it. It was what he said that people should do about it that caused the trouble. Similarly, the significant part of the message of Jesus for us may lie here, in the imperatives; for, as we have just seen (p. 20), the statement that the end was near was not fulfilled.

REPENT

The word which Mark uses is μετανοεῖν, but the translation Repent is misleading. To us, to repent suggests to be sorry for something one has done; to feel regret or penitence about something. The Greek word, however, has the primary meaning, To change one's mind; to decide to do something different from what one had been going to do. It is used in this sense, for example, in the Greek version of Jonah, where God changes his mind about destroying Nineveh; the king of Nineveh says: Who knows, God may yet repent and turn from his fierce anger, so that we perish not? And the story goes on:

When God saw what they did, how they turned from their evil way, God repented of the evil which he had said he would do to them; and he did not do it.   *(Jonah 3. 9)*

To repent, here in Jonah, means to change your mind; to change course. And the same is true in Mark. This is perhaps why the first imperative (repent) is followed by another (believe in the gospel—or better, believe in the good news) which defines the meaning of the first more precisely; the way in which they are to change course is through believing the good news. And part of this good news, though only part, as we shall see later, is that the kingdom of God is at hand.

So much for the imperatives in the Marcan summary of the message of Jesus. The question now is, Does this summary (Repent, and believe the good news) help us to link together and understand some of the sayings of Jesus?

THE KINGDOM AND REPENTANCE

The first point is obvious, but even so it must be made: if it is *God* who is going to rule, then there will be no scope for private empires. If *God's* name is about to be hallowed, and *God's* kingdom about to come, and *God's* will about to be done, both in heaven and on earth (such is the meaning of the phrase in the Lord's Prayer, Matt. 6. 9f), then there will not be any space left anywhere for self-willed, disobedient, recalcitrant beings.

To use an analogy which Jesus does not use: it is like what you do (if I understand it aright) if you are in a sailing boat in a very strong wind: you present the narrowest aspect of the boat to the wind; if it catches you on the side, you will capsize. Similarly, Jesus says that the alternatives are repentance and salvation, or no repentance and destruction. See, for example, Luke 13. 1f, and the repeated saying:

Unless you repent you will all likewise perish.

Though Jesus does not use this analogy, he uses a number of metaphors which are very similar, and come to the same thing in the end. For example, he uses the idea *smallness*:

Enter by the narrow gate; for the gate is wide and the way is easy, that leads to destruction, and those who enter by it are many. For the gate is narrow and the way is hard, that leads to life, and those who find it are few.   *(Matt. 7. 13f)*

The follower of Jesus must be small in order to fit through the narrow gate and survive in the time when God rules; if he is too big he will not get through.

Exactly the same idea of smallness comes in the famous saying:

It is easier for a camel to go through the eye of a needle than for a rich man to enter the kingdom of God.   *(Mark 10. 25)*

This is an exaggeration, or hyperbole; Jesus was always using them. ("Always", here, is another example of hyperbole!) There is no evidence for a small gate called the Needle's Eye, through which it was just possible to get a camel. And the saying has nothing to do with the difficulty of threading camel-hair. These are the inventions of capitalist commentators. Jesus means, It is impossible to get a camel through a needle: just so, it is impossible to get a rich man into the kingdom of God. The reason is, because he is too big: he has too much power; this power will not be able to withstand the infinitely greater power of God. He will therefore capsize. The only hope for a man is smallness—that is, powerlessness.

The same idea is expressed by a different symbol in a saying which is found a number of times in the gospels:

Many that are first will be last, and the last first.
                        (Mark 10. 31, cf. Matt. 20. 16, Luke 13. 30)

That is to say, those who are first in importance in this age will
be last in the age to come, and those who are of least importance
in this age will be the first in the age to come. (Notice here the
future tense, Will be; it is an eschatological future and it refers
to the way things will be when God rules. There are many
cases of the use of the future in this way in the saying of Jesus;
see, for example, the Beatitudes, Matt 5. 4–9.)

There is a similar detached saying which comes more than
once in the Gospels:

Every one who exalts himself will be humbled, and he who humbles
himself will be exalted.
                              (Luke 14. 11, cf. Matt. 18. 4; 23. 12; Luke 18. 14)

Notice here, that, as well as the future tenses which refer to the
age to come (will be humbled; will be exalted), the verb is also
passive (be humbled; be exalted). These passives are further
examples of devout periphrasis (see above, p. 14), and they
mean that God will act:

God will relegate, down to hell, the man who promotes himself in
this age;

God will promote, in his kingdom, the man who relegates himself
in this age.

This saying is placed after the parable about choosing places
of honour at a marriage feast (Luke 14. 7f); this parable is not
a piece of sound advice for those who are socially uncertain (it
is not an extract from a treatise on etiquette), but it is as Luke
says a *parable*, and it is about the kingdom of God and how to
live in order to enter it: Put yourself in the lowest place now,
and when God comes in judgement, he will say to you, Friend,
go up higher.

Similar ideas are expressed in the sayings of Jesus concerning children:

Let the children come to me, do not hinder them; for to such belongs
the kingdom of God.

Truly, I say to you, whoever does not receive the kingdom of God
like a child shall not enter it.   *(Mark 10. 14f)*

The point is not that children are good at receiving presents; or that they are naive or humble: they are not. (These interpretations are the inventions of commentators who either were celibates, or employed nannies). The point is that children have no status; they are no better than slaves, as Paul says (Gal. 4. 1); the ancients were not sentimental about children. Jesus used the child as the model of the disciple, because the child was a nobody. Again, it is the idea of smallness, unimportance, powerlessness, inferiority, being last.

Part of what Jesus meant by repentance is this: God is going to rule, so you had better abdicate. Turn from your usual course into the opposite direction. Your usual course is self-aggrandisement: the opposite direction is self-abnegation. There are many sayings of Jesus in which this theme comes. For example: 1. The sayings about *forgiveness*. To forgive is to forgo one's rights; not to forgive is to stand upon one's rights. The disciple is to have no rights; they would make him too big to fit through the narrow gate. So we have, for example,

If you forgive men their trespasses, your heavenly Father also will forgive you [in the last judgement]; but if you do not forgive men their trespasses, neither will your Father forgive your trespasses.
(Matt. 6. 14f; see also Matt. 18. 21f, Mark 11. 25)

2. Similarly, the sayings about *giving*; for example,

Give to everyone who begs from you; and of him who takes away your goods do not ask them again.   *(Luke 6. 30)*

Go, sell what you have, and give to the poor, and you will have treasure in heaven [i.e. in the sight of God]. . . How hard it will be for those who have riches to enter the kingdom of God!
(Mark 10. 21, 23)

3. Another kind of wealth is *respect*. A man can try to make himself secure in this age by amassing goods, or he can try to do it by accumulating respect from other people. Jesus is as much against the one as the other. This is why we have,

Beware of practising your piety before men in order to be seen by them; for then you will have no reward from your Father who is in heaven.   *(Matt. 6. 1)*

This principle of no respect now in order to have a reward in the kingdom in the future is then exemplified in three ways: almsgiving; prayer; fasting (Matt. 6. 2–18). And the section is rounded off with this conclusion:

Do not lay up for yourselves treasures on earth... but lay up for yourselves treasures in heaven [i.e. in the sight of God].

(Matt. 6. 19f)

4. Finally, this aspect of repentance is stated most fully and completely, when Jesus says that his disciples must deny themselves, and lose their lives.

If any man would come after me, let him deny himself and take up his cross and follow me. For whoever would save his life will lose it; and whoever loses his life for my sake and the gospel's will save it. For what does it profit a man, to gain the whole world and forfeit his life? *(Mark 8. 34f)*

To deny oneself does not mean what we understand by self-denial—giving something up (cigarettes; sugar). To deny oneself means to disown oneself; to admit no connection with oneself. It is the word used when Peter denies Jesus during the trial before the Sanhedrin (Mark 14. 30f, 72). Similarly, to take up one's cross does not mean to accept an inconvenience (a physical defect; a tiresome relative); it means capital punishment, death.

The aspect of repentance which we have looked at so far is that which is expressed by the symbols: smallness, poverty, child, death, etc. But there is more to repentance than this. Jesus does not mean that the disciple is to do nothing. He means precisely the opposite. He is to be fully active—doing the will of God.

When God's kingdom comes, his will will be done. The only possibility of anyone other than God existing in God's kingdom is if he does God's will. Nothing else will be able to exist; otherwise it would not be *God's* kingdom.

So we have, for example:

Whoever does the will of God is my brother, and sister, and mother.

(Mark 3. 35)

A man had two sons; and he went to the first and said, Son, go and work in the vineyard today. And he answered, I will not; but afterward he repented and went. And he went to the second and said the same; and he answered, I go, sir, but did not go. Which of the two did the will of his father?   *(Matt. 21. 28f)*

Repentance is therefore turning from self-will to obedience to the will of God. And this will of God claims a man's obedience in such a way that it leaves him with no area of his own, no privacy. The man who wishes to enter God's kingdom must see himself as entirely at God's disposal; so, for example, in this parable:

Will any one of you, who has a servant ploughing or keeping sheep, say to him when he has come in from the field, 'Come and sit down at table'? Will he not rather say to him, 'Prepare supper for me, and gird yourself and serve me, till I eat and drink; and afterward you shall eat and drink'? Does he thank the servant because he did what was commanded? So you also, when you have done all that is commanded you, say, 'We are unworthy servants; we have only done what was our duty'.   *(Luke 17. 7f)*

Jesus says that to enter the kingdom you must do God's will; and to do God's will is to reckon upon a demand made upon you that will be so great that it will leave you nothing for yourself. Therefore, like the man who wants to build a tower, the disciple must first sit down and count the cost; and like the king going to war with another king, the disciple must sit down first and take counsel; because

Whoever of you does not renounce all that he has cannot be my disciple.   *(Luke 14. 28f)*

And the same point is made in the two parables of the treasure and the pearl:

... he goes and sells all that he has and buys that field.
... went and sold all that he had and bought it.   *(Matt. 13. 44f)*

Repentance, therefore, has two sides to it, a negative side, and a positive. The negative is described by means of the analogies of smallness, lowliness, poverty, and death; the positive is obedience to the will of God. The self-will of the disciple is to die; his will is to be completely occupied in doing God's will.

If the question were asked, "Did Jesus define the will of God? Did he tell his disciples what to do?" part of the answer would be that he did not. He certainly did not give them detailed instructions—a new code, by which to live in obedience to God. He did not define God's will, partly because he believed that the Law of Moses gave them all that they needed. When somebody asked, "What must I do to inherit eternal life?" he answered

You know the commandments: 'Do not kill, Do not commit adultery, Do not steal, Do not bear false witness, Do not defraud, Honour your father and mother'.   *(Mark 10. 17f)*

He also said:

If they do not hear Moses and the prophets, neither will they be convinced if some one should rise from the dead.   *(Luke 16. 31)*

And he taught, as others also taught, that there were no commandments greater that the commandment to love God, and to love your neighbour as yourself (Mark 12. 28f). But there may be another reason why Jesus did not give his disciples more detailed instructions: he believed that people do in fact know what God's will is; they are able to judge for themselves. His use of parables shows that he assumed that it was possible for people to see things for themselves: his parables invited his hearers to make comparisons and to reflect on the stories in order to perceive God's will. Jesus was, we might say, extremely optimistic; and like many optimists was often disappointed:

He looked around at them with anger, grieved at their hardness of heart.   *(Mark 3. 5)*

THE MIRACLES AND REPENTANCE

The point we have reached so far is this: Jesus said, Repent; to repent means to change the direction of your life. Jesus said, Stop doing your own will and do God's will; and God's will is doing good (i.e. love).

What we shall see now is that once again (see above p. 19) the actions of Jesus fit in with his words and serve the same purpose.

By his actions, what is meant here is his miracles. The healing miracles were a call to repentance: they declared the beginning of God's rule and were therefore a demand for a change of attitude. The proper response to the miracles was not wonder or amazement, but repentance. Jesus did not do miracles in order to show people who he was, but in order to show them what time it was: that the end was near; and by this, to call them to the kind of life which was appropriate for such a time:

Then he began to upbraid the cities where most of his mighty works had been done, because they did not repent. "Woe to you, Chorazin! woe to you, Bethsaida! for if the mighty works done in you had been done in Tyre and Sidon, they would have repented long ago in sackcloth and ashes. But I tell you, it shall be more tolerable on the day of judgement for Tyre and Sidon than for you. And you, Capernaum, will you be exalted to heaven? You shall be brought down to Hades. For if the mighty works done in you had been done in Sodom, it would have remained until this day. But I tell you that it shall be more tolerable on the day of judgement for the land of Sodom than for you".   *(Matt. 11. 20f)*

That is to say, the mighty works of Jesus (i.e. the healing miracles) called the people of Chorazin, Bethsaida, and Capernaum to repent, in order that they might pass through the judgement when it came on the last day (and thus quite soon). But they had not repented; therefore Jesus said they would be destroyed.

BELIEVE THE GOOD NEWS

We saw above (p. 18) that *part* of the good news (Mark 1. 15) in which Jesus called for belief was that God was going to rule. But it is now clear that this was only part. Because by itself, the news that God is going to rule is not good—except for saints. For everybody else (or in fact, one might say, for everybody) the coming of God's rule is very bad news. This is how it is for the rich man in the parable in Luke 16. 19f; and for the rich fool in the parable in Luke 12. 16f; and for the man who hid his master's money in the ground (Matt. 25. 14f; cf. Luke 19. 12f); and for the improvident bridesmaids on whom the door was shut (Matt. 25. 1f).

Again and again, Jesus says Woe!, warning people of the coming cataclysm, in which the first will be last, the rich poor, the happy miserable, the exalted lowly.

If the beginning of God's rule means the end of man's freedom to sin, and if all men are sinners, then the coming of God as king is not good news at all.

And yet this is not the impression we get of the message of Jesus as a whole. It is not all gloom and destruction; there is joy and happiness in it. We cannot therefore have got it right, yet. What is left out?

What is missing is a complete range of ideas contained in the tradition of the sayings of Jesus concerning God and God's attitude to people; and in the tradition of the actions of Jesus, concerning the way in which he lived and behaved.

The news that God is going to rule is good news, only because it is *God as Jesus proclaims him* who is going to rule. The demand which Jesus makes upon his hearers, in the name of God, is accompanied with an assurance about God, which Jesus gives both in word and deed; and this assurance about God makes it possible for his hearers to face the demand.

An obvious example of the teaching about God which Jesus gives is the picture of the father in the parable of the Prodigal Son (Luke 15. 11f). The point is that the father treats the younger son as a son and not as a servant; he welcomes him back with rejoicing, not with condemnation, and treats him with mercy, not with justice. And the same theme comes in the two parables which Luke puts before this: the Lost Sheep and the Lost Coin (Luke 15. 3f); in both of them, the owner looks for his lost property and rejoices when he finds it. Jesus is saying that God's attitude to people is like that. He will not grumble about them, or find fault with them; he is too happy over finding them for that; they are his property and belong to him. And this is the case, whether they are worthy of it or not.

The good news is that the God who is going to rule is the God who owns the world and is merciful and loving towards it; he is the one whom Jesus calls Father (Abba) and teaches his disciples to address in the same way.

Again it is important to remember the miracles of Jesus, because it is in *healing* miracles that Jesus demonstrates the coming of God's rule, not in destructive plagues (as at the time of the Exodus), nor in calling down fire from heaven (as in the case of Elijah, 2 Kings 1), nor in cosmic disasters (as in Joel 2. 30f). The healings which Jesus performs bear witness to the mercy of the God whom Jesus proclaims.

We shall look at this subject again in the next section. Meanwhile, the point to notice is that Mark's summary of the imperatives of Jesus (Repent, and believe in the good news) has provided us with a way of assembling the material in the tradition and making coherent sense out of it. Repent, because it is God who is going to rule; Believe that it is the God who is your Father who is going to rule.

3

4   THE OFFENCE OF JESUS

There has been a type of Christian devotion which has made much of the idea that it would have been wonderful to have known Jesus in the days when he lived as a man among men; to have walked with him beside the lake of Galilee; to have listened to his parables; to have watched him as he healed the sick; to have seen his face as he prayed. It is summed up in the exclamation, O that we were there!

It seems to me that this way of thinking is both presumptuous and misinformed: the majority of those who met Jesus did not like him at all; what are we assuming, if we think that we should have been among the few who believed what he said and obeyed him?

Jesus said,

Blessed is he who takes no offence at me. *(Matt. 11. 6 = Luke 7. 23)*

He was not one who brought peace, but a sword:

I have come to set a man against his father, a daughter against her mother, and a daughter-in-law against her mother-in-law; and a man's foes will be those of his own household.
(Matt. 10. 34f, Luke 12. 51f)

He was a contentious person: for ever arguing with people, particularly with those in authority; hated by the religious leaders of his people, and eventually put to death. If Mark's account of the ministry is anything to go by, he was often not understood by his followers either: they were amazed, afraid, terrified. Jesus was frequently rebuking them and reproving them; he was always mystifying them.

Thus, whether we had been devout Jews like the Pharisees, or members of the religious outcasts who eventually became his followers, there is no reason to think that we should have enjoyed any privilege through being a contemporary of Jesus. We should have found him as insufferable and intolerable as they.

The question we must consider now is, What was so offensive about Jesus? What was it that made people hate him so much that in the end, apparently, they had him killed? How did Jesus get across the Jews?

These questions are not easy to answer. First of all, the evangelists give us very little help here. Mark, for example, begins his passion narrative with this introduction:

It was now two days before the Passover and the feast of Unleavened Bread. And the chief priests and the scribes were seeking how to arrest him by stealth, and kill him; for they said, "Not during the feast, lest there be a tumult of the people". *(Mark 14. 1f)*

At this point in his Gospel, at least, Mark provides no explanation why the chief priests and scribes took this step. Later, he will say that Pilate perceived that it was out of envy that the chief priests had delivered him up (15. 10); earlier, he had told the story of the cleansing of the temple, and the parable of the tenants of the vineyard, and after each of these he had said that the authorities wished to arrest Jesus and destroy him (11. 15f, 12. 1f). But apart from these and a few similar remarks elsewhere in the Gospel (e.g. 3. 6), Mark does not provide his readers with any clear and explicit statement of the issue between Jesus and the Jewish leaders, such as would account for their decision to condemn him. In this respect, as in so many others, Mark, and the other evangelists like him, do not satisfy what we expect from a biographer. Why is this so?

1. The opposition between Christians and Jews at the time when these Gospels were written (*c.* A.D. 65–95) was sufficient explanation for the readers. They knew how much the Jews hated *them*: no wonder they had hated their Lord in time past. There was no need to preserve in the tradition a statement of the historical issues between the Jewish leaders and Jesus; and what was not needed was not preserved.

2. The first disciples probably had no access to the discussions of the authorities which led to their decision to arrest Jesus and try him. So that even if the Christians had wanted to know

about this, it is unlikely that they would have had any means of doing so.

3. In any case, they were much more interested in a different aspect of the matter, namely, in the providence of God, who, they believed, had ordained and declared in the scriptures that the Messiah must suffer. They were more interested in theology than in history. Hence if they had wanted to know the historical reasons for the death of Jesus, and had been able to find them out, they would not have been of any great interest to them. The important point, as they saw it, was that God had intended it, and that the scriptures had foretold it. It had all happened in order that the scriptures might be fulfilled.

But there is another obstacle in our way. If what we want is to find out why Jesus and the Jewish leaders got across one another, we have to reckon with this difficulty: we only have one side of the story—the Christians' side. This means, not only that we cannot use any Jewish evidence (because there is none), but also that the material we have in the tradition in the Gospels and elsewhere in the New Testament is prejudiced and distorted. All the material we have comes to us from people who believed in Jesus as Saviour and Lord; that is to say, it comes from people who, in one sense, no longer found Jesus offensive. And this means that his original offensiveness has been obscured and overlaid by the faith of those who passed the tradition on. Therefore we get from the Gospels a weakened and diluted impression of the contentiousness of Jesus. He must have been more offensive than the Gospels suggest. What was this controversy about?

JESUS' AWARENESS OF HIMSELF AS IN OPPOSITION

One of the facts which seem to be clear from the tradition is that Jesus was conscious of himself as an outsider. He saw himself as one who was in opposition to the religious leaders of his time, and his message as a message that would not be accepted by the majority of his contemporaries.

It comes, for example, in the parable of the sower, the seed, and the different kinds of ground into which the seed falls:

A sower went out to sow.
And as he sowed, some fell along the path, and the birds came and devoured it.
Other seed fell on rocky ground, where it had not much soil, and immediately it sprang up, since it had no depth of soil; and when the sun rose it was scorched, and since it had no root it withered away.
Other seed fell among thorns and the thorns grew up and choked it, and it yielded no grain.
And other seeds fell into good soil and brought forth grain, growing up and increasing and yielding thirtyfold and sixtyfold and a hundredfold.   (Mark 4. 3f)

The point of this parable is clear from its form. It tells two stories—the story of unproductive ground, and the story of ground which is productive. But it tells the first story three times—on the path; on rocky ground; among thorns. It tells the second story once. In a sense therefore it would be true to say that the emphasis of the parable is on the failure of seeds to grow—though the final section of the parable shows that this failure is wholly offset by the abundance of the yield from the good soil.

Whatever the original setting and purpose of the parable (and it is not clear what they were) this aspect of it cannot really be doubted: it contrasts apparent and repeated failure with ultimate success. And this may have been the meaning of it as it was originally used: Jesus was aware of his inability to convince the majority of his hearers of the truth of what he was saying.

A similar contrast between failure and success is to be found in the parable of the invitations to the marriage feast:

They would not come.
They made light of it.
The wedding is ready, but those invited were not worthy.
                                              (Matt. 22. 2f)

And again in the parable of the Good Samaritan: the first man to go along the road is a priest, and he passes by; the second is a Levite, and he also passes by. The man who acts is not the one you would expect next (i.e. an Israelite layman) but a Samaritan (Luke 10. 30f). Similarly, there is the parable of the Pharisee and the tax-collector, where it is the tax-collector who is justified, not the Pharisee (Luke 18. 9f); and the tenants in the vineyard, who reject the servants of the owner (Mark 12. 1f); and the elder brother in the parable of the Prodigal Son (Luke 15. 11f); and the labourers in the vineyard who complain and grumble at the payment of those who were hired last (Matt. 20. 1f).

In all of these, and in more of them, Jesus shows that he is aware of the opposition between his message and the Jewish leaders. They are offended at what he says, and he knows it.

The same theme appears in other parts of the tradition; for example, in the *sayings*. There are the woes on Chorazin, Bethsaida, and Capernaum (Matt. 11. 20f, see above, p. 29). There are warnings such as

Beware of the leaven of the Pharisees and the leaven of Herod.
(Mark 8. 15)

Beware of the scribes.   *(Mark 12. 38f)*

There is the Matthean section of woes on the scribes and Pharisees (Matt. 23). In these too we have evidence of Jesus' understanding of the conflict between himself and the religious leaders of Judaism. He sees himself as one who is in opposition; his teaching is against the stream.

The purpose of going into this at some length may not be obvious. It might have been thought that it is perfectly clear that Jesus and his message were rejected by the Jewish leaders, because we know that he was crucified. The death of Jesus proves the point, without any further evidence.

The reason for not taking this short cut was because according to some writers it is not a safe route; it is not at all certain, they say, that the Jews were responsible for the crucifixion of Jesus. Certainly crucifixion was not the Jewish way of dealing with offenders: their method was stoning; crucifixion was how the Romans did it. Therefore it has been suggested that Jesus was put to death by the Roman authorities for political reasons, either because he was a political menace, or because he was thought to be a political menace, rather than because of his actual teaching and its offensiveness to the Jews.

The purpose of going through the material in the tradition which shows Jesus as one who was aware of himself as in opposition to his religious contemporaries was in order to by-pass this problem. Even if the decision to put Jesus to death was a political act of the Roman authorities in Jerusalem, it still remains the case that Jesus was in conflict with the Jewish leaders. Therefore we can still ask, What were the issues involved? What caused the friction between him and them?

TWO MATTERS WHICH WERE NOT THE CAUSE OF FRICTION

In order to clear the ground before we begin to answer this question, we shall consider two areas which might have been thought to be areas of friction, and to have provided reasons why the Jews rejected Jesus.

1. *Jesus' claims about himself.* It has been suggested that Jesus claimed a position for himself, and used titles of himself, and that he was rejected for this reason. For example, that he said that he was the Messiah, or the Son of God; and that this was blasphemy.

This is indeed the impression which the reader of John's Gospel receives; and this is what the synoptists say in their accounts of the trial of Jesus before the high priest. Commentators say that we must treat the latter with great caution. But in any case, the trial took place *after* the arrest, and after the decision to arrest Jesus; whatever took place then could not account for what happened before. Moreover, it was not blasphemy to claim to be Messiah or Son of God. (On the historical value of the Fourth Gospel, see above p. 12).

We shall consider the claims of Jesus in the next section; all I intend to say now is that in my view, and in that of many of the writers on this subject, it is highly unlikely that the Jewish leaders decided to put Jesus to death because he claimed, explicitly, to be the Messiah.

2. *Jesus and the Law of Moses.* Another suggested reason for the conflict might be that Jesus' teaching was in opposition to

the Mosaic Law. This is also an impression that might well be gained from reading the Gospels, particularly Mark's gospel. There is there, for example, the section in which Jesus argues with the Pharisees over the law of clean and unclean, and, according to Mark, he declared all foods clean (Mark 7. 1f).

Here again we must be very careful. It may well be that Mark is reading back into the situation before the crucifixion, the attitude and beliefs of *some* Christians of his day—attitudes and beliefs which arose only after the resurrection, and perhaps outside Judea.

This again is a difficult question; but it does seem to be the case that, if Jesus had been as critical of the Law as Mark says in this passage, it would be hard to understand why some Christians continued to observe the Law after the resurrection, and claimed the authority of Jesus for doing so; for example:

The scribes and Pharisees sit on Moses' seat; so practise and observe whatever they tell you.   *(Matt. 23. 2f)*

Certainly on a matter such as contact with Gentiles, Jesus seems to have been very much of the view that it was not for him to have dealings with them; for example:

I was sent only to the lost sheep of the house of Israel.
                                                       (Matt. 15. 24)

The Law of Moses made the distinction between Jews and Gentiles, and Jesus observed it. He did not ride rough-shod over the Law.

Therefore, if the conflict between Jesus and the Jewish leaders was not caused by his claim to be Messiah or Son of God, or by his total disregard for the Mosaic Law, what were the causes of it?

THE OFFENCE OF THE MESSAGE OF JESUS

The answer seems to be that Jesus caused offence through being critical of the Law in a far more subtle way than by abrogating it completely. Jesus' teaching was that the Law was inadequate, as a statement of the will of God. He called men to repent and to do the will of God; he also said that to do the will of

God was not identical with doing what the Law commanded. The point is made in the story of the rich man. Jesus says:

You know the commandments: 'Do not kill, Do not commit adultery, Do not steal, Do not bear false witness, Do not defraud, Honour your father and mother'.

and the man replies:

Teacher, all these I have observed from my youth.

Then Jesus says to him:

You lack one thing; go, sell what you have, and give to the poor, and you will have treasure in heaven; and come, follow me.
(Mark 10. 17f)

That is to say, exact fulfilment of the Law does not constitute the kind of obedience which God demands. There is more to obedience than the fulfilment of the commandments.

Exactly the same point is made in the story of the Pharisee and the tax-collector. The Pharisee is speaking the truth when he says:

God, I thank thee that I am not like other men, extortioners, unjust, adulterers, or even like this tax-collector. I fast twice a week, I give tithes of all that I get.   *(Luke 18. 11)*

Moreover, he is attributing his obedience to God by thanking God for it. But this is not the obedience that Jesus demands. The Pharisee was not justified; the tax-collector who said "God, be merciful to me a sinner" was justified. Obedience to God is not the same thing as obedience to the Law: obedience to the Law makes it possible (as the Pharisee shows) to trust in oneself that one is righteous and despise others; the obedience that Jesus demands is more searching and exhaustive than any law could ever be, and it leaves no place on which to stand and look down on other people.

This understanding of the nature of thoroughgoing obedience comes again in the antitheses in the Sermon on the Mount:

You have heard that it was said to the men of old, 'You shall not kill. . .'. But I say to you that everyone who is angry with his brother shall be liable to judgment. . . .

You have heard that it was said, 'You shall not commit adultery.' But I say to you that everyone who looks at a woman lustfully has already committed adultery with her in his heart. . .
You have heard that it was said to the men of old, 'You shall not swear falsely. . .'. But I say to you, Do not swear at all. . .
You have heard that it was said, 'An eye for an eye and a tooth for a tooth.' But I say to you, Do not resist one who is evil. . .
You have heard that it was said, 'You shall love your neighbour and hate your enemy.' But I say to you, Love your enemies. . .
You, therefore, must be perfect, as your heavenly Father is perfect.

(Matt. 5. 21f)

The criticism that Jesus made of the Law was more subtle than a simple, straightforward repudiation of it. What he was saying was that commandments do not produce complete obedience to God. It is possible to keep to the rules, and at the same time disobey God, still not love God. The demand of God is for an obedience which is thoroughgoing, and leaves no room for self.

Criticism of the Law of that kind, in that situation, would produce hatred of the one who made it, because one of the by-products of having a law and of obeying it is a sense of security, satisfaction, and looking down on other people ("I thank thee that I am not like other men"). To attack this is to attack a man's self-respect, and this is to injure him at his most sensitive point. Jesus' offence was that he taught that the will of God was more than obedience to the Law.

WHY WAS THIS GOOD NEWS?

However, we cannot stop here, because, if that was all that Jesus said, it would not have been good news. If he had simply come with the news that God expects more of men than even the Pharisees had thought, this would have been no good news at all. There must have been more to what Jesus said than a re-statement of the demand of God, in more exacting terms.

The strange thing is that what Jesus said in this respect was also totally offensive to the Jewish leaders. He was in conflict with them on two fronts: first, in that he demanded more from men (in the name of God) than the Law had done; secondly, in that he proclaimed a God who was more merciful than the God implied by the Law.

One of the facts which comes out of a study of the tradition about Jesus is that he ate and drank with tax-collectors and sinners; that he chose his companions from those who were not Pharisees; and that he defended his choice of this company with teaching concerning the mercy of God. It is with God, he said, as with a sheep-owner who searches for a lost sheep; or as with a woman who searches for her lost coin; or as with a father who welcomes home a lost son (Luke 15). When the older brother complains that he has served his father for many years and never disobeyd his command, the father replies that commands and service are not the way of thinking about the relationship between father and son: All that is mine is yours (Luke 15. 31).

The relationship between God and men is not that of master and servants, or of Law and commandments, but of owner and property, parent and child. And this may be the reason why Jesus uses the unusual word *Abba* of God—unusual in this context, apparently; possibly even unprecedented in Judaism; a word expressing the relationship of a small child to his father. And this may be the point of the parable of the Labourers in the Vineyard: the owner pays the last men a full day's wage, because they must live and he is generous; he is not bound by any law that forbids him to do what he chooses with his own property (Matt. 20. 1f). But it is made clear beyond all doubt in these sayings:

What man of you, if his son asks him for bread, will give him a stone? Or if he asks for a fish, will give him a serpent? If you then, who are evil, know how to give good gifts to your children, how much more will your Father who is in heaven give good things to those who ask him!   *(Matt. 7. 9f)*

Finally, this is precisely the point of the prayer of the tax collector in the parable: he simply says, "God, be merciful to me a sinner!" All he does is, he asks; he throws himself upon God's mercy; and he is justified (Luke 18. 9f).

This is why the message of Jesus is good news. If God is to
be thought of in this way, then it is possible to live without care;
it is possible not to be anxious about tomorrow (Matt. 6. 25f).

And this is also why the message of Jesus caused offence to
the Pharisees and the scribes. They are depicted in the com-
plaining older brother and the grumbling labourers who had
worked all day in the burning heat. If God is as generous as
Jesus says, they can have no special claim upon him. God is the
Father of the tax-collectors and sinners, as well as of the pious,
and there are no particular relationships in his family. His
goodness is free, and it is for all; it is not limited by merit or
deserts. The proclamation of the mercy of God, like the
proclamation of his demand, undermines the security of the
Pharisee.

THE DEMAND AND THE MERCY OF GOD

There is one more point to notice here, namely, how these two
elements in the message of Jesus fit together—the demand of
God for thoroughgoing obedience, and the assurance of God's
unlimited mercy and generosity.

At first sight there might seem to be a contradiction between
them, and they might appear as alternatives: either God is
totally demanding, or he is utterly merciful. But in fact it is not
so. Experience shows that it is not possible to take the demand
of God seriously (and not go mad), unless his mercy is also
asserted and believed. And it is not possible to believe in the
mercy of God (and not go bad), unless his claims and demands
are maintained rigorously. The only viable procedure is to say,
Nothing is good enough for God; but he will accept whatever
I do, however small and unworthy it may be.

This is the way in which we would wish to treat our friends,
and our families. We want to do the best for them; we say that
they deserve everything that is possible. But we know that our
relationship with them is not conditional upon our performance.
We believe that our friends will remain our friends, even if we
should let them down.

The offence of Jesus lay in this: he spoke of God as Father,
and he taught that the relationship of God with men trans-

cended that which is implied by the Law. It went beyond the Law in two directions: on the one hand, God's demand is greater than that of the Law; on the other hand, God's mercy is wider than that involved in rewarding men according to their deeds. His teaching was offensive on both counts: it undermined the security provided by obedience to the Law, and in this way attacked the self-confidence of the Pharisees; it opened the kingdom to those who were not strict in their keeping of the Law—the tax-collectors and sinners—and in this it ruled out complacency.

For this doubly offensive teaching, Jesus was hated by the Jewish leaders—and should be hated still by any who think about God as they did.

5 THE AUTHORITY OF JESUS

The picture of Jesus which emerges from the Gospels when historical criticism is used is very different from the impression of him which is received when they are read uncritically. It is like the children's books of forty years ago, which had illustrations in different colours; when you put a piece of coloured transparent paper over the page it cancelled out some of the lines, and an entirely new picture stared at you. In the same way, historical criticism of the Gospels produces a different impression of Jesus from the traditional picture. They differ in two respects: (i) in regard to what seems to have been the message of Jesus; (ii) in regard to what Jesus seems to have said about himself.

1. *The Message of Jesus.* The idea that the centre of his message was the belief that the present world-order was coming to an end soon is a comparatively recent discovery, made about the turn of this century. Early on, in New Testament times in fact, the eschatological orientation of the message of Jesus began to be obscured; notice, for example, how Luke refers to Jesus in one of the speeches in Acts:

God anointed Jesus of Nazareth with the Holy Spirit and with power; . . . he went about doing good and healing all that were oppressed by the devil, for God was with him.   (*Acts 10. 38*)

Luke omits completely from this description of the activity of Jesus any reference to him as the one who preached the coming of the end. The same process has gone further in the fourth Gospel, where the characteristic term which Jesus used, the kingdom of God, appears only twice in the whole book (John 3. 3, 5).

It is not difficult to see why this was so: to have said that

Jesus expected the end to come soon when it was known that it did not, would have caused as much difficulty then as it does now.

2. *What Jesus said about himself.* Here again there is a vast difference between the traditional view and what many present-day writers on the subject are saying. The traditional view has been that Jesus made great claims for himself; that he said that he was the Messiah, the King of Israel, the Son of God, the one who existed with God before Abraham, the eternal pre-existent Word of God.

That Jesus made claims for himself of this kind was assumed in the popular argument: Either he was God, or he was a wicked person. It was said, Jesus claimed that he was divine; either he was or he was not; if he was, he was; if he was not, he was either bad or mad; does whatever else we know about Jesus suggest that he was either of these?

But as soon as critical methods are applied to the Gospels, explicit claims to divinity begin to disappear. For example, it is noticeable that the most prominent claims are in John's Gospel only; all the I AM sayings are Johannine, and there is no exact parallel to them in the synoptics.

The titles which are used of Jesus by the synoptists are often in the *redaction* rather than in the *tradition*. The *tradition* is the material which the evangelists received, and it usually came to them in small units: parables, miracle-stories, sayings. The *redaction* is the editorial work of the evangelists, linking the units together. The titles of Jesus in the synoptic Gospels are frequently part of this editorial work. So, when the redactional elements are removed, and the traditional units are recovered in the form in which they came to the evangelists, there is a lower density of titles. For example, these two passages in Mark are part of his redaction:

The beginning of the gospel of Jesus Christ, the Son of God.
(Mark 1. 1)

Whenever the unclean spirits beheld him, they fell down before him and cried out, 'You are the Son of God'. And he strictly ordered them not to make him known. *(Mark 3. 11f)*

In the same way, many writers would regard the birth and infancy stories in Matthew and Luke, with their comparatively frequent use of titles (the King of the Jews, the Christ, the Son of the Most High) as in part redactional, and in part legendary, material which has very little historical basis. The same would be said about the accounts of the temptations, and the predictions of the passion and resurrection.

It is not difficult to see what happened, or why it happened. Those who handed on the stories after the resurrection believed that Jesus was the one who was soon to come again in glory as the judge and king of the age to come. What they believed about his future influenced the way in which they described his past; they talked about his life in Galilee and Judea as if it had been messianic and retrojected the picture of what he would be on to the tradition of what he had been. Or to put it another way: it has been said that "no man can recall past events without being affected by what has happened in between".[1] When Christians recalled the ministry of Jesus, they could not but be affected by their belief that, in between, Jesus had died and been raised up and exalted to God's right hand. The process can be observed as it happens, when the Fourth Gospel is compared with the synoptists, and when Matthew and Luke are compared with Mark; it is then possible to extend the lines backwards and distinguish between historical and legendary material even in Mark.

The conclusion to which this kind of investigation points is that Jesus did not speak of himself as the Messiah (=the Christ); that he did not claim to be, in a unique sense, The Son of God; and that he did not use the title the King of Israel of himself. If he used any title, it was the Son of man, but even this is not certain: he may have been referring to some one other than himself who was to come in the future.

It seems that Jesus did not apply labels to himself; but that, if he had been asked what he was, he might have said Prophet and he might have said Teacher. Apparently these two titles

---

[1] A. J. P. Taylor, reviewing J. C. C. Davidson, *Memoirs of a Conservative*. Ed. by Robert Rhodes James in the *Observer*, 31 August 1969, p. 20.

were used of him: people addressed him as Teacher and described him as a prophet.

The reason for putting this in the hypothetical form (if he had been asked... he might have said) is because the tradition suggests that Jesus was not much concerned to talk about himself; he was too concerned to talk about something else, the Kingdom of God. The whole point of his message was to say, God is going to rule, and he is going to do so very soon; therefore change the direction of your life, and do it in this way. His message was not about himself, but about God.

Notice in this connection the beginning of the story of the rich man; he addresses Jesus as Good Teacher:

"Good Teacher, what must I do to inherit eternal life?"

And Jesus said to him, "Why do you call me good? No one is good but God alone."
(Mark 10. 17f)

It is very unlikely that this is not original, and highly probable that it is authentic. It is not the kind of answer that a later Christian would put into the mouth of the Lord; in fact we can see what a later Christian writer made of it, by looking up the parallel in Matthew:

"Teacher, what good deed must I do, to have eternal life?" And he said to him, "Why do you ask me about what is good? One there is who is good."
(Matt. 19. 16f)

It seemed impossible to Matthew that Jesus should have rejected the title Good Teacher, so he rewrote the passage.

The conclusion to which these arguments lead us is that it was not the intention of Jesus to proclaim himself or to attract attention to himself, but to proclaim God's rule and attract attention to God. Therefore it is not surprising if he did not use messianic titles, or indeed any other titles, with reference to himself.

However, this way of putting it is not adequate, and we shall return to it later. Meanwhile, we must consider another aspect of the problem.

4

THE AUTHORITY OF JESUS

A fairly common type of argument may be set out as follows:

    X says so and so;

    X is an authority on this subject;

    Therefore we must follow X's advice in this matter.

A slight variation of this is when X is the speaker; here the pattern is this:

    I say so and so;

    I am an authority on this;

    Therefore you must do what I say.

Now the interesting thing is that we do not find this kind of argument in the tradition concerning Jesus. We do not find him appealing to faith in himself as Teacher, Prophet, Messiah, or Son of God, in order to give authority to his teaching. He did not demand faith in himself as the pre-condition of receiving his message, or use his status to authenticate what he said. That is to say, he did not lord it over his listeners. And this is in line with what he is said to have taught his disciples:

You know that those who are supposed to rule over the Gentiles lord it over them, and their great men exercise authority over them. But it shall not be so among you; but whoever would be great among you must be your servant, and whoever would be first among you must be slave of all. For the Son of man also came not to be served, but to serve, and to give his life as a ransom for many.

(Mark 10. 42f)

We might reach the same conclusion if we said that Jesus saw himself as a teacher. There are two alternative directions in which a teacher can turn for authority: he can either say, I have studied the subject for many years; got degrees and diplomas in it; written books on it; therefore I am to be believed; or he can say, Look at the matter for yourself; can you not see that these facts point to this hypothesis; that A is more likely than B; that that thesis must be wrong because it does not fit in with the data?

The first of these is a false kind of authority, and ineffective, because it binds the pupil to the teacher, and blinds him to the subject. The second is the genuine authority, because it liberates the pupil, and opens his eyes to the subject under discussion.

The authority which Jesus used seems to have been of the second kind, rather than the first. He saw himself as a teacher; and the teacher, according to this second way of thinking, is in the end dispensable. He only occupies a position temporarily; he holds it because he began to study the subject earlier in time than the pupil; and eventually the pupil will arrive there for himself. This seems to be the meaning of these sayings:

Can a blind man lead a blind man? Will they not both fall into a pit?
A disciple is not above his teacher, but every one when he is fully taught will be like his teacher.   (*Luke 6. 39f*)

Jesus, as teacher, directed the attention of his hearers to the will of God. He expected them to recognize it for themselves and to obey it because it was evident to them—not because he said it. And this is the only way in which it is possible to be completely and freely obedient. We can see this in the story about his mother and his brothers:

'Who are my mother and my brothers?' And looking around on those who sat about him, he said, 'Here are my mother and my brothers! Whoever does the will of God is my brother, and sister and mother.'   (*Mark 3. 33f*)

He did not see himself as occupying a unique and exclusive position into which no one else could come. He saw himself as a point around whom others could cluster, and with whom they could be associated: the family of those who do the will of the Father.

Moreover this kind of authority fits in with what we know about the method of teaching which Jesus used. He taught in parables. The purpose of teaching in parables is to make it possible, by means of simile and metaphor and analogy, for the hearer to see the truth for himself. A parable is an aid to insight. Jesus taught in order that his hearers might share his insight.

This brings us back to the inadequate statement above (p. 47): It was not the intention of Jesus to proclaim himself or to

attract attention to himself. . . . After all, did he not say, Follow
me? The fact that he taught means that he did in one sense
attract attention to himself. No one can teach unless those who
are to be taught attend to him. Jesus clearly did demand attention, both by teaching and by performing miracles of healing.

But there is no contradiction here; or rather, the contradiction is present in the teaching of Jesus. It is expressed in the
antithesis: me/not me. For example:

'Whoever receives one such child in my name receives me; and
whoever receives me, receives not me but him who sent me.'

(*Mark 9. 37*)

Jesus saw himself as the one sent by God to declare the
coming of God's kingdom. His authority was entirely from
God. To believe in him was to believe in what he stood for. He
lived out of God, and for God; and in calling people to follow
him, he was calling them to live out of God, and for God: poor
in spirit, meek, mourning, hungry and thirsty for righteousness.
He did in a sense believe in himself, as any teacher must, or
else he cannot be a teacher. But he believed far more in his subject, as any teacher must. And Jesus' subject was God's
kingdom.

THE AUTHORITY OF JESUS FOR US

We might now return to a problem which has been with us at
various points in these pages (e.g. pp. 21f, 44f). The title of this
section is The Authority of Jesus, and so far we have been
considering the kind of authority he claimed and the manner in
which he exercised it. But the question might well be asked,
Has Jesus any authority *for us*? Has he anything to say to
people now?

At first it might seem as though the answer must be No.
Subsequent events proved that his message was wrong. The
kingdom of God did not come then, and still it has not come.
He said that some standing there in Palestine with him would
not taste death before they saw the kingdom of God come with
power (Mark 9. 1), but they all died and the new age had not
arrived. Surely this must falsify everything else that he said.

His message, according to Mark's summary, was "The time is fulfilled and the kingdom of God is at hand; repent, and believe in the gospel" (Mark 1. 15), but we know now that it was not at hand; therefore nothing that he said can have any authority for us. What is there to be said about this?

Perhaps there is only one thing that needs to be said about it: the conclusion (nothing that he said can have any authority for us) does not follow from the premise (Jesus was wrong about the imminence of the end). It is entirely possible for people to come to a true understanding of themselves, and of what they should do, in circumstances about which they are in error. It happens every day.

For example, a man might be told by his doctor that he had only six months to live; and he might decide on the basis of this information to make his will, pay his outstanding debts, put his affairs in order, live charitably, and devote more time to prayer. Would he then feel that he had wasted good opportunities, if instead of six months he were to live another six years, or sixty?

The situation in which Jesus taught men concerning the will of God was created by the preaching of John the Baptist: belief in the nearness of the end. But this belief was only the historical factor that triggered off his teaching. His message can stand, apart from the truth or falsity of this belief. The question "Was Jesus right about the will of God?" is an entirely separate question from "Was he right about the nearness of the end," The idea that the world was coming to an end soon was the setting in which Jesus operated; it is necessary for us to understand the setting, if we want to make sense of what he was saying. But what he said in his historical context may still be valid for people who do not accept the premises from which he started.

The belief that the world was coming to an end is not the only piece of first century Jewish culture accepted by Jesus which we do not and cannot share with him. Others are: Mosaic authorship of the first five books of the Old Testament; the Davidic authorship of the Psalms; and the idea that demons are the cause of various kinds of sickness. Eighty years ago

Bishop Gore argued, in his essay in *Lux Mundi*, that Christians must accept that Jesus thought in these first century ways. What is being said now is that the area covered by the human knowledge of Jesus may have to be enlarged beyond what was thought then. Jesus was wholly, fully, and completely a first century Jewish man. Is it desired that he should not have been?

Therefore there is no need to give up faith in Jesus because he thought that the end was near. It is what he made of first century ideas that matters, not the ideas he started from.

The question, Has the message of Jesus any authority for us? depends on our decision about his message: does what he said make sense of life to us? This was the only kind of authority that he recognized. Judge for yourselves!

If the argument and conclusions in the previous pages are at all on the right lines, they will present the Christian of today with a problem. The purpose of this final chapter is to say what the problem is, and to suggest one way in which it might be treated.

To put the matter as crudely as possible, Does it not seem to be the case that we are dealing with two people, both of them called called Jesus? On the one hand there is the first century man, who lived in Galilee and Judea, thought as a Jew, and was very different from us. And on the other hand there is the Lord who is with us, the one in whom we believe, who tells us what to do and enables us to do it, assuring us of our forgiveness when we fail. How are we to relate the one to the other? What does our knowledge of the first century man contribute to our understanding of the present Lord? And what does our knowledge of the present Lord contribute to our understanding of the first century man?

It may help to clarify this problem if we look at the causes of it. There seem to be two: *faith*, and an interest in *history*.

If we do not *believe* that Jesus is Lord now, it would be a simple matter to abandon him to the historian, and cut the knot in that way. There is no problem in thinking about other first century men, because they are not the object of faith and hope and love. It is because Jesus is, for the believer, not only a man of the past but also Lord in the present, that the believer has his problem.

Secondly, if we were not interested in *what happened*, we could solve the problem in another way: we could rewrite the Gospels, in order to express what we believe about Jesus, and take no more thought for the past. This was, to some extent, the solution of the first century Christians: Matthew and Luke rewrote Mark; John replaced the synoptists. If we had no interest in history, we could think of Jesus as he is for us, as if he was the Jesus who lived in Palestine.

The problem for the present day Christian is that of the continuity between Jesus as he was then, in the first century, and as he is now (the Lord); and the discontinuity between the two. A sense of history compels us to see the difference: we cannot think of him as if his thoughts at that time were like ours today; but on the other hand, faith compels us to assert the continuity: the one in whom we put our faith is identical with the one who taught in Galilee and died outside Jerusalem.

It may be that we can get somewhere towards a solution of this if we ask the question, What happened between then and now? How did Jesus pass from being a first century man to becoming the Lord in whom men believed and continue to believe?

There was only one event that caused the change: Resurrection from the dead. And in order to think about this, it will help if we use what Paul said about the resurrection of the body:

What is sown is perishable, what is raised is imperishable.
It is sown in dishonour, it is raised in glory.
It is sown in weakness, it is raised in power.
It is sown a physical body, it is raised a spiritual body.

(1 Cor. 15. 42f)

Paul could speak derogatively about the body—that it is perishable, dishonourable, weak, merely physical—because he believed that the body was to be raised, imperishable and glorious, powerful and spiritual. He was not tempted to idolize the body of flesh—because he believed in its future destiny. Similarly, if we believe in the resurrection of Jesus, we can face the fact that in the days of his flesh he was different in many respects from what he is now. He was wholly and completely a first century man.

But it happens in the reverse direction too: Paul, believing that the body of flesh and blood is to be raised, and is for the Lord, teaches with conviction that it is not for fornication. Its future destiny controls and determines how it is to be used now. In just the same way, what we know of Jesus now, as he meets us as our Lord, is related to the way in which he met men in the days of his flesh. He comes to us now with the demand of God for obedience, and with the assurance of God's mercy to sinners; and this is how he met men in Galilee and Judea in the first century.

The way in which the believer thinks of Jesus in the present is filled out and made concrete by what he can discover about Jesus in the first century. The believer knows him as the one who comes to him with the command to love, and with the assurance of forgiveness—yet this is how every man knows him without knowing him, because forgiveness and love are common to all men. What the believer has that others have not is the name to give to the one who comes to him in this way; he can put a face on him.

The way in which the believer studies Jesus as he was in the first century will be different from the way in which others study him: the believer is studying one whom he has already met, so he knows what to look for; the Lord, in whom he believes, is the same person as the man who spoke in parables and healed the sick. The believer has a clue to what he meant then, because he knows what he means now; this should save his research from dullness.

BIBLIOGRAPHY

GENERAL

G. Bornkamm, *Jesus of Nazareth* (Hodder 1960)
R. Bultmann, *Jesus and The Word* (Fontana 1962)
H. J. Cadbury, *The Peril of Modernizing Jesus* (S.P.C.K. 1962)
H. J. Cadbury, *Jesus, What manner of man* (S.P.C.K. 1962)
M. Dibelius, *Jesus* (S.C.M. 1963)
J. M. Robinson, *A New Quest of the Historical Jesus* (S.C.M. 1959)
H. Zahrnt, *The Historical Jesus* (Collins 1963)

THE KINGDOM OF GOD

N. Perrin, *The Kingdom of God in the Teaching of Jesus* (S.C.M. 1963)

THE PARABLES

J. Jeremias, *The Parables of Jesus* (S.C.M. 1963)
J. Jeremias, *Rediscovering the Parables* (S.C.M. 1966)
E. Linnemann, *Parables of Jesus* (S.P.C.K. 1966)

THE MIRACLES

R. H. Fuller, *Interpreting the Miracles* (S.C.M. 1963)

THE LORD'S PRAYER

C. F. Evans, *The Lord's Prayer* (S.P.C.K. 1963)
J. Jeremias, *The Prayers of Jesus* (S.C.M. 1967)
E. Lohmeyer, *The Lord's Prayer* (Collins 1965)
J. Lowe, *The Lord's Prayer* (Oxford 1962)

SOME OTHER RELEVANT BOOKS

C. K. Barrett, *Jesus and the Gospel Tradition* (S.P.C.K. 1967)
E. Fuchs, *Studies of the Historical Jesus* (S.C.M. 1964)
R. H. Fuller, *The Foundations of New Testament Christology* (Fontana 1969)
E. Käsemann, *Essays on New Testament Themes* (S.C.M. 1964)
E. Käsemann, *New Testament Questions of Today* (S.C.M. 1969)
J. Knox, *The Death of Christ* (Fontana 1967)

BIBLIOGRAPHY

J. Knox, *The Ethic of Jesus in the Teaching of the Church* (Epworth 1962)
N. Perrin, *Rediscovering the Teaching of Jesus* (S.C.M. 1967)
N. Pittenger (Ed.), *Christ for Us Today* (S.C.M. 1968)

The following books were published after these lectures were written:

E. Käsemann, *Jesus means Freedom* (S.C.M. 1969)
H. K. McArthur, *In search of the Historical Jesus* (S.P.C.K. 1970)
N. Perrin, *What is Redaction Chriticism?* (S.P.C.K. 1970)
J. Reumann, *Jesus in the Church's Gospels* (S.P.C.K. 1970)